£6

The Isle of ...

A POSTCARD TOUR

VOLUME TWO – DOUGLAS AND THE EAST

compiled by

Steven Dearden and Ken Hassell

DOUGLAS HARBOUR I.O.M.

Richard Stenlake Publishing
1996

ACKNOWLEDGMENTS

The pictures on pages 1, 8 (top), 27 (bottom), 44, 45, 49 (top), 55 (bottom), 59 (top), 79, 80 and 88 (top) appear courtesy of S.R. Keig Ltd of Douglas under whose copyright they remain. Many thanks to the firm for their kind permission for inclusion.

Lhen Coan Station at Groudle (not Sea Lion Station as the caption on the card says!)

INTRODUCTION

The second in our series on the Isle of Man, this volume covers Douglas and the East of the island in the years between 1900 and 1939. Volume one featured Ramsey and the North and future volumes will cover Castletown and the South and Peel and the West. All the cards illustrated are drawn from our two collections.

At the beginning of the twentieth century photography found a key place in communications between ordinary people. Family portraits, events, places, all were recorded and the images were very much in demand, not only to meet the needs of communication, but also to satisfy the postcard collecting fever of this century's first decade. In the period between 1900 and 1914 the Isle of Man had well over half a million visitors a year and the vast majority of those numbers would have sent a record of their holiday to friends and relatives, all in the form of postcards. As a result Manx photographers were much in demand throughout the island, particularly around Douglas, and fortunately this area was serviced by highly skilled exponents of the trade. When looking at the photographic postcards of this period, a knowledge of those who produced them is very helpful.

Outstanding in the history of Isle of Man photography is the firm of S.R. Keig, Ltd, founded in 1861 by Thomas Keig, who was also the first Mayor of Douglas. His successors in the photographic business were his son Thomas and his grandson, Stanley, and it is thanks to those two that so many events in the first half of the century have been documented and recorded so well. The family tradition continued through Stanley's son Nicky, and the firm is now owned by Timothy Keig, great-great-grandson of its founder.

The firm of Keig were not, however, the only photographers at work during this period. Competition was keen and notable amongst the others was Louis Henry Taggart who did some excellent studies at Groudle. Photographers who mainly restricted themselves to portrait work were Fred Johnson, W.H. Warburton, Miss M. Kirton, and Stafford Johns. W. Comery also worked during this time, going out to the villages around Douglas and capturing scenes that were rarely depicted on the mass-produced cards published by the major national companies.

Deserving of special mention is David Collister (1857 - 1930). Originally from England, he married Mary Jane Bridson from Douglas and by the early 1880s was fully established in his trade. When Cunningham's Camp was opened in 1905 on the Little Switzerland site he gained the position of Official Photographer. There, with the help of his sons, he had to cater for the requirements of an average 4000 campers per week, most of whom wanted a record of their stay. In addition to the photographic business, he also owned a boarding house in Douglas, 'Pentlands' at 1 Waverly Crescent, which was not only the family home but also catered for many visitors under the management of Mary Jane. After Collister's death, the photographic business was run by his son Harry until 1939.

This compilation celebrates the work of these photographers and the invaluable record of their times which they left. We would also like to thank David Bailey, Bob Dowty Jnr and Alan Kelly for the invaluable information that they have supplied, and also the staff of the Manx Museum Library for their assistance.

Steven Dearden and Ken Hassell.

David Collister sitting in his favourite deckchair at 'Pentlands'.

At the beginning of the century the first taste of the island for its millions of visitors was the journey on one of the vessels of the Isle of Man Steam Packet Company. Of no exception was one Mr DeLoose, his wife, mother and daughter, who visited the island in 1907. DeLoose was the general secretary of a firm called Royce Ltd which was based in Manchester. Both he and the firm were soon destined for Derby where the company would be renamed Rolls Royce. The island was not a random choice for the DeLoose's holiday as his employers, C.S. Rolls and H. Royce, had serious business interests there in promoting their new cars by having them compete in the recently established Tourist Trophy race.

Like their fellow travellers, the family would have enjoyed the bracing sea journey. However, they also had the luxury of a cabin, together with the attention of a cabin attendant.

Mrs DeLoose, her daughter and cabin attendant.   Interior of Isle of Man Steam Packet Co. cabin.

The acquisition of a cabin also gave the family more space than was usual, although playing cricket would not be the norm - a case of 'six and out' perhaps?

Victoria Pier, packed with holiday-makers arriving, departing or just sight-seeing.

Once in Douglas the DeLoose's took part in all the activities enjoyed by thousands of tourists . . .

. . . having their photographs taken with the donkeys on Douglas shore . . .

. . . watching lawn tennis in the Palace grounds . . .

. . . and joining the heaving throng on Douglas Head being entertained by the Pierrots.

The period between 1907 and the beginning of World War Two was one of significant change for Douglas and the surrounding area. The gallery of photographs on the following pages document many of the buildings, streets and scenes from that time which were lost to new developments.

By 1935 the Visitors' Information Bureau in Douglas was a prominent feature of the triangular Victoria Pier arcade. Forrester's Dining Rooms were at the other end, with shops all around and a pleasant seated area in the centre with a fountain and tropical plants. The Angle Clock was a local landmark and crowds would be addressed from the flat arcade roof on special occasions. The Royalty Cinema and Peveril Hotel are directly behind the Clock.

David Kewley (1850 - 1904) was one of the Steam Packet Company's boatmen and is said to have saved no less than thirty-five men from drowning over the years. Familiarly known as 'Dawsey', he received the Royal Humane Society's bronze medal and the publication of this card on his death gives an indication of the esteem in which he was held. In his memory, a drinking fountain bearing his likeness was constructed at the head of the Victoria Pier buildings.

Keigs produced this postcard showing the civic reception for the visit of the Archbishop of Liverpool to Douglas in June 1929. The mayor, Alderman William Quirk, seems to have met the visitor actually on the Steam Packet vessel. On his visit, Archbishop Downie also visited Ramsey and a card showing his visit there is included in volume one of this series.

Prior to 1926 buses were banned from using the promenade and visitors would travel to their seafront hotel by horse trams which were often double deckers. That year, however, the trams stopped for the winter and have operated a seasonal service ever since. This is the entire single decker fleet of Douglas Corporation buses at the time, although the fleet had grown to thirty-one only three years later.

BALLOON ASCENT AT DOUGLAS

On 10 November 1902, the first balloon flight on the island took place. A week previously the equipment had been transported by *HMS Renard* under the supervision of the famous aeronaut Percival Spenser (whose family manufactured the balloons) and another enthusiast, Rev. J.M. Bacon. The Douglas gasworks had been ordered to stand by with 45,000 cubic feet of gas and while preparations were made Rev. Bacon gave two lectures on the benefits of aviation at the Gaiety Theatre. His suggestion that it might offer a viable alternative for sufferers of seasickness was greeted with some amusement by the sceptical audience.

On the morning of the 10th, 15,000 spectators gathered in favourable weather to see the balloon take off from Peveril Square and as a matter of safety those on the windward side were banned from smoking by the police. The flight safely commenced at 1.34 p.m. and ended in Dumfriesshire four hours later. The photographs taken from the balloon provided the very first aerial views of the island for non-flyers, but the main object of the flight was to test signalling equipment and the balloon remained in contact with *HMS Renard* throughout.

Built to link the new Victoria Pier with the developing part of the town, the Loch Promenade was completed in 1875, further extensions seaward being added in 1930. In this 1920s Lilywhite photograph the Saturday afternoon crowds, just arrived off the boats, mill around the Jubilee Clock. Stafford Johns' photographic studio is on the right.

The immediate post-war period saw a variety of victory celebrations in Douglas, including a carnival and a homecoming reception at the Nunnery for the returning servicemen. As the holiday trade began to return to normal, celebrations continued into 1920 with the building of this archway at the Victoria Pier end of the Loch Promenade to mark a further victory carnival. A highlight of that year was the two day visit by King George V and Queen Mary in July.

The inner harbour had many of the oldest buildings in town, some of which dated back to the early eighteenth century when the port began to develop trading in tanned hides, salted herring, timber, beer and coal. Nearly all the warehouses have now been demolished, although some of the older property has been converted into small business units.

Always a bustling place, the Quayside was never more busy than when the fishing boats came in and their catches were laid out on the ground near the Market Place to be auctioned to fishmongers and hoteliers. The original swing bridge of 1895 is visible in this Stengel view from 1905. Pedestrians were charged a ha'penny to cross while workmen living on the Head side, or needing to travel to work at the gas works were issued with free passes.

When the fishing fleet was in it was sometimes possible to walk right across the harbour on the decks of the vessels. To the right are berthed a harbour ferry and the paddle steamer *Ben-my-Chree II* which is resting at the Tongue, a regular winter berth for Steam Packet vessels. Following reboilering in 1884 and the fitting of two additional funnels, the *Ben-my-Chree* became the only four funnelled ship in the company's history; she was broken up at Morecambe in 1906. The large schooner at the North Quay would probably be unloading timber from Norway for Quiggin's Saw Mills on the nearby Lake Road.

Built in 1840, the *Success* became a prison hulk in Melbourne Harbour in 1853 and after years of disuse was fitted out as a touring exhibit, eventually arriving in Douglas harbour in 1911. The convict ship was visited by thousands to view the cells, figures in irons and relics such as the cat-o'nine-tails. While she was at the island an American, David H. Smith, persuaded a group of local businessmen to buy her and the vessel remained in their hands until 1922, touring America until she was destroyed by fire in 1946.

Fort William, on the Douglas Head road, offered holiday accomodation with a fine view but slightly removed from the crowded promenades. Guest houses there included the Grosvenor, Rhodes House, Werneth House and Fort William House. Local photographer Fred Johnson had his studio at No. 8 - taking care that his trading sign was clearly visible from across the harbour. This is one of his postcards from 1905.

The Fort Anne Hotel was one of Douglas's most prominent landmarks and its demolition in 1979, only for the site to be left derelict, is one of the more extraordinary planning decisions of recent years. Built in 1792 by Irishman Buck Whalley, the foundations were laid in specially imported soil in order to comply with the terms of his wife's inheritance - that she should live on Irish soil. Before the building became a hotel, the founder of the RNLI, Sir William Hillary, lived there from 1825.

When bringing your car to the island in 1909 there were no 'roll-on/roll-off' facilities. Before 1914 the Battery Pier was the scene for many arrivals such as the one above.

By 1930 cars were a common sight, and perhaps more exciting for sightseers was the arrival of a squad of British submarines, captured on film by Stafford Johns.

The steam ferry boats *Rose*, *Shamrock* and *Thistle* ferried holidaymakers across the outer harbour to the Battery Pier from about 1900 to the 1950s. The fare was 1d each way and queues could be six deep for the three or four minute service. Musicians, including a pianist, would entertain on the short passage and visitors needed little encouragement to join in the choruses.

The *Mona* was built as the *Hazel* for the Laird Line, being acquired by the Steam Packet Company in 1919 for use on the cargo and winter passenger service. Stafford Johns took this photograph in July 1930 when she became stranded on the Conister Rock in thick fog. Passengers and cargo, including a race horse and animals for a circus at Laxey, had to be unloaded into another ship before *Mona* could be towed off by the tug *Strongbow* with the help of coasters *Ben Veg*, *Texa* and *Staffa*. The face of the Victoria Pier was painted white as a result of the incident to make it more distinctive in poor light.

In June 1924 Keigs photographed the *Peel Castle* after it ran aground in fog in Douglas Bay off Broadway. Fortunately, the *Fenella* was able to tow her off on the rising tide without serious damage. Built in 1894, the *Peel Castle* was originally named *Duke of York* before being bought by the Steam Packet Company in 1912. After serving as an armed boarding vessel between 1915 and 1918, she remained in service until 1939, being particularly associated with the direct Liverpool-Ramsey sailings in her later years.

BATTLESHIPS IN DOUGLAS BAY

The visit of the First Division of the Channel Fleet was a highlight of 1907. The fleet included six battleships and two cruisers and the Douglas boatmen did good business taking sightseers out to view the ships. A regatta, sporting events and a searchlight display were among the events organised. The sender of this card writes enigmatically, 'having a fine time - nearly married!'

BATTLESHIPS IN DOUGLAS BAY
H.M.S. BRITTANIA   H.M.S. HINDUSTAN

The crew were also allowed some of the fun and five hundred of them were taken on a visit to Ramsey by the railway and cricket matches were organised. The fleet stayed from the 1st to the 5th of August and the sailors were allowed into most entertainments in Douglas at half-price, providing that they were in uniform.

The lifeboat house in this Baur's postcard is the old structure on the Battery Pier, replaced by the current boathouse in 1924 when the first motor lifeboat arrived. This particular building only dated from 1896 and was completed for the arrival of the new lifeboat shown here, the *Civil Service No. 6* which served until the motor boat was introduced. To launch the *Civil Service*, it had to be dragged across the road to the slipway,

Lifeboat House, Battery Pier, Douglas. I.o.M.

a not inconsiderable feat for a forty-two foot long boat weighing eleven tons. When the boat returned from an action twelve horses had to be borrowed to pull it back up the slipway.

LAUNCHING THE LIFEBOAT AT DOUGLAS

The considerable speed that the boat developed on the slipway before hitting the water can be seen in this Keig's card. Problematically, the slipway was exposed to easterly winds which meant that when the boat returned from service it sometimes had to be taken to the inner harbour where it was stranded at low tide. The *Civil Service No.6* saved forty–eight lives during her years of service.

The 200 yard stretch from the foot of the incline railway down to the ferry crossing at the harbour was always extremely busy and boasted many attractions to separate visitors from their money. However, very long hours had to be worked by the various traders - the oyster bar, for example, only closed after the last trippers had descended from the Head and reopened before breakfast to catch the first bathers on their way to Port Skillion.

Port Skillion was built by Robert Archer in 1874 as a bathing place for gentlemen and was possibly the first open-air pool in Britain. Many female admirers attended, much to the consternation of the moral guardians of the time, but splendid accomodation for diving and swimming was offered, as well as 'towels, bathing drawers and lock-up dressing rooms'. By the time this Sands postcard was produced mixed bathing was allowed and the pool remained popular until it was badly damaged in a storm in 1932.

Douglas Head still offers the best view to be had of the town, although there is no longer such a wealth of activity to be seen. This card dates from 1911 and shows some of the amusement stalls at the foot of the incline railway. The funicular railway, built in 1900, can just be seen behind the boy on the left. The steamers at the pier include the *Snaefell III* of 1910 which was torpedoed and sunk in the Mediterranean in 1918.

The Channel Fleet in the bay during its visit of 1907, a year before the fog signal was added to the Douglas Lighthouse. The first light on Douglas Head was erected by the Harbour Commissioners around 1832 and was rebuilt in its present form in 1892. At 104 feet above the high water mark, its 132,000 candle power light was recognisable fourteen miles out as it gave its signal of six quick flashes in fifteen seconds followed by fifteen seconds of darkness. The lighthouse is now fully automated, with a signal flashing every ten seconds.

Song publisher Bert Feldman made his fortune with 'It's a Long Way to Tipperary' but after the war he turned impresario, focusing his attentions on Blackpool and the Isle of Man. His community singing rooms on Strand Street and the promenade were packed on wet days and he also leased the concert party pitch on Douglas Head, where Feldman's

Songsters are performing in this view from June 1925. The 6d 'Blue Book', containing Feldman songs such as 'Flanagan' and 'Has Anybody Here Seen Kelly?', sold in its thousands.

The Great Union Camera Obscura on Douglas Head was built in 1887 by a Rochdale man, James Fielding. Now closed and in need of preservation, its unique feature is that it has eleven viewing turrets rather than just one. This allowed a constant flow of people through the building at busy times and made it very popular for watching the thousands of courting couples on the Head who thought they were hidden from view.

The years between 1896 and 1939 saw the operation of the Douglas Head Marine Drive Electric Tramway. This W.A. Camwell photograph shows car No. 7 at the Port Soderick terminus in the tramway's final year of operation. Car No. 1 survives at the Crich Tramway Museum but little remains of the line except for the entrance gates to the Marine Drive.

Port Soderick was developed after the coming of the railway by the Forrester brothers and at the height of its popularity boasted many stalls and side shows, including a camera obscura like the one on Douglas Head. Above is one of the more unexpected attractions, serving the double purpose of demonstrating the freshness of the milk served in the restaurant and putting on a pastoral show for town dwelling tourists who had probably never been so close to a cow.

At the rear of these Port Soderick beach buildings is the Crogga river which flows through the surrounding glen. Amusements and arcades continue to mark the area, but prior to the last war the arcade had a more curious attraction - the padded cell from the hospital of the *Olympic*, sister ship of the *Titanic*.

An elevated iron walkway took visitors from the beach to the oysterbeds and the smugglers' caves. The Forrester family advertised Port Soderick as the only 'free glen' on the island - but money still had to be made and stalls on the beach sold candles for visitors to explore the caves, some of which extend hundreds of yards into the hillside.

The parish church of St Matthew the Apostle on Douglas Quay was designed in the early English style by the architect John Loughborough Pearson. Replacing the famous old chapel of St Matthew in the Market Place nearby, the church was completed in 1907.

The Grand Theatre on Victoria Street featured comic operas and music hall acts, and the complex of buildings also incorporated a bowling alley and sea water swimming baths. The Grand became the Regal Cinema and in 1977 a bank.

OLD DOUGLAS, SENESCHAL LANE.   OLD DOUGLAS, BOND STREET.

Seneschal Lane and Bond Street were amongst the oldest of Douglas's streets in 1911. Bond Street housed the famous Step Down public house, which before the quay became built up, was on the very edge of the shore. The whole area of old Douglas was demolished in the 1930s.

The Old Curiosity Shop presents a strange sight with its collection of stuffed animals, freaks and old weapons. Even stranger was the fact that it was not a shop at all; clues to its real identity can be seen in the piano and advertisements for Martell Brandy and Okell's Ales. The establishment is now better known as the Derby Hotel on Castle Street.

Before its development in the 1930s, with the growth in traffic and the building of the Pulrose estate, the Peel road was the start of a favourite country walk. The road was very narrow, particularly where it passed the allotments and gardens known as Hills Meadow, and near the junction with Belle Vue Road was 'Mammy' Kneen's shop where refreshments were available to walkers on the way to the Nunnery or Kirk Bradden. The Brown Bobby pub was one of the local landmarks lost to the road-widening scheme.

A view of Douglas station, predating the erection of the platform canopy which was begun in December 1908. The impressive size of the items of luggage is a reflection of the long holidays some families would spend on the island. The railway was still extremely busy at this time with over a dozen trains travelling each way on each line during the summer.

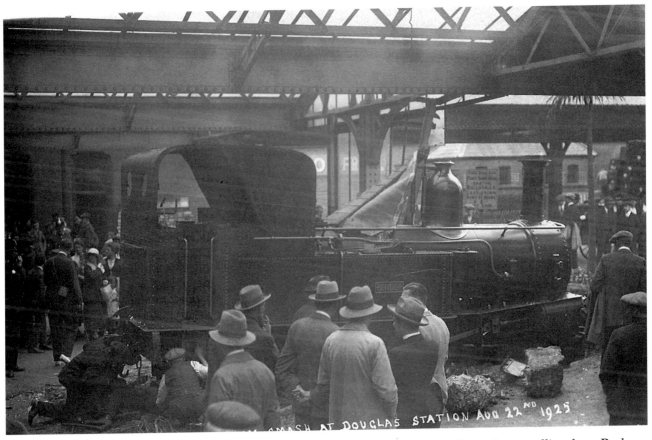

This accident was probably the most spectacular in the local railway's history. The train, travelling from Peel, left Union Mills without its guard or brakesman and on reaching Douglas the driver, who was unaware of this, found he had insufficient brake power to stop. Although the train smashed into the buffers, only one passenger was badly hurt. However, the fireman of the train had jumped clear before impact and later died of his injuries. As can be seen here, the engine travelled to within six feet of the station building before stopping.

This Foden steam wagon at the Quarterbridge depot was bought by the Highway Board in 1920 and was the first such vehicle to be seen on Manx roads. It could carry five tons, ten times as much as a horse and cart, and served into the 1950s before being sold to a local farmer. Years later its remains were used to rebuild a similar wagon in England.

Sir William Drinkwater was one of the first car owners on the island and the first president of the Manx Automobile Club when it was formed in 1905. Behind him here is the Nook Refreshment Gardens and the Quarterbridge Hotel. The Quarter Bridge, over the River Glass, took its name from its location at the junction of four roads and is a popular vantage point on the T.T. course today.

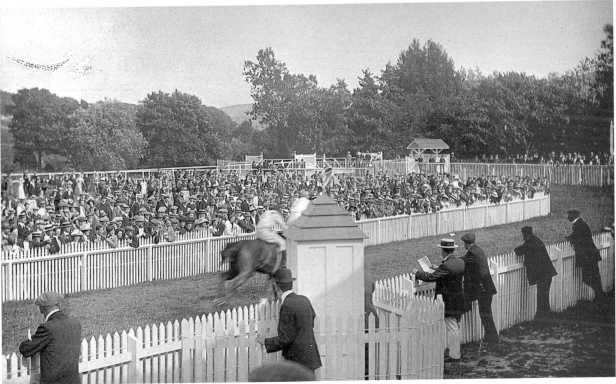

Belle Vue, originally laid out as an athletics stadium in 1889, became a racecourse in 1912 even though the old course at the Strang was still in use. The races were very popular and horses were brought over for the whole season to race before the thousand-seater grandstand. The course closed in 1931 following difficulties with the authorities regarding course-side betting, but four years later the ground was reopened as King George V Park and is now the site of the National Sports Centre.

In 1903 Douglas was still surrounded by large Victorian estates and prosperous farms such as Pulrose (left). Pulrose Manor House, to which the farm belonged, was long associated with the Moore family, but passed into the hands of Douglas Corporation in 1927. The area was completely changed by the resulting housing developments.

A hunt gathers at the Nunnery, although there was nothing larger on the island to persecute than a hare. The Nunnery mansion only dates back to 1820 when General Goldie pulled down a house built by the Heywood family, which formerly stood on the site. It was in the old house that Peter Heywood, midshipman on the *Bounty* during the mutiny, was born. The present mansion was designed by John Pinch in the style he popularised in Regency Bath known as Strawberry Hill Gothic.

The Fourteenth World Manx Association Gathering taking place in the grounds of the Nunnery in 1924. Visitors from the United States, South Africa, New Zealand, Australia, Ceylon and Canada were all present.

This interior view of St Bridget's Chapel at the Nunnery dates from 1935 and shows the restoration work carried out in 1881. The chapel is one of the oldest on the island still in use, dating in parts from as early as the thirteenth century. It is the only part of the ancient Nunnery which remains.

Old Kirk Braddan appears here little changed from when it was built in the 1770s. It houses a collection of runic crosses of which Thorleif's, which was used as the model for the Braddan War Memorial, is particularly striking. The larger new church was built nearby in 1876 but the old church continued to be used, and open air services were held in the churchyard until 1913.

Up to 35,000 people attended the Kirk's open-air services and for many years special trains operated to a nearby railway halt. The origin of the custom dates to June 1856 when a sermon by Bishop Powys was attended by so many people that many could not get into the church. The practice continued after 1913 when accomodation for the crowd was provided at the spacious fortification above the new church.

RETURNING FROM SUNDAY SERVICE AT KIRK BRADDAN, I.O.M.   96462.JV.

CORNER OF BANNISTER'S SHOP,
DUKE ST. DOUGLAS.

This card was sent by one of the Bannister's shop assistants to her friend, proudly proclaiming where she worked. However, visitors would have been more likely to go to the many shops selling souvenirs such as Webb's Bazaar. Crested china, Manx teapots and other 'presents from the Isle of Man' are now much sought after by collectors.

Although Bent's Florists was situated on Finch Road, Mr Bent was better known for selling fashionable posies and button holes from a pitch between Gaiety Theatre and Villa Marina, or in the mornings at the Palm Court entrance to Cunningham's Camp. Excellent business could be done in the evening as holidaymakers passed on their way to the theatres and dance halls.

The Maypole Dairy Company shop was situated on the corner of Howard Street and Strand Street and is now occupied by a travel agents. All the shop's produce was individually wrapped and their speciality was 'Mayco', a mixture of butter and margarine. The shop was also noted for the decor of green and white picture tiles showing rural scenes covering the inside walls and floor.

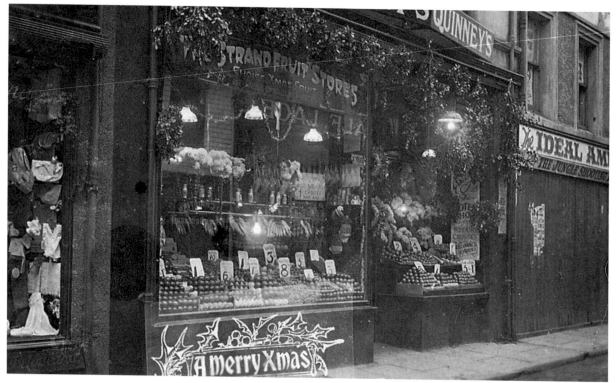

A Christmas display at Quinney's Strand Fruit Stores. The Ideal Amusements next door are closed for the winter, a seasonal aspect of Strand Street that has lessened in recent years.

Strand Street appears here to be in carnival mood with festive bunting much in evidence. The authors would be very pleased to receive any more information regarding this card.

Strand Street with one of Douglas's popular restaurants in the foreground. Other frequented cafes in town included Collister's on Victoria Street and Collinson's in Duke Street, both now closed.

Rapid developments took place in the island's postal services following the transfer of control in 1886 to the expanding Liverpool District. A new headquarters was constructed and in 1887 staff were able to move from Athol Street into the handsome red-brick building leading immediately off the new Loch Promenade.

The Methodist Church on Victoria Street was built in 1878, and demolished in 1977. Afterwards, the site was occupied by Barclays Bank. The Park Road Secondary School premises were around the corner.

Having become the island's capital in 1874 it was necessary for Douglas to find suitable accomodation for the House of Keys and members of Tynwald. After its failure the Bank of Mona's buildings, dating from 1854, were used for this purpose, the Legislative Buildings being completed in 1894. The year of the bank's closure, 1878, had been marked by a sensational incident in which the chief cashier had attempted to rob the branch of £8,873 in gold.

St George's Church prior to extensive alterations carried out in 1909-10. The oldest church in Douglas, it was built in 1780 with the support of local merchants and gentry who were looking for a 'more convenient and elegant place of publick worship'. Notable graves in the churchyard include those of Nellie Brennan, who gave her life nursing cholera victims in the 1830s, and Sir William Hilary, founder of the Royal National Lifeboat Institution.

Private schools prospered on the island well into the current century. Victoria College on Victoria Road advertised itself as offering a 'thorough preparation for the professions and for commercial purposes' and the curriculum included an impressive list of English, French, Greek, Drawing, Advanced Mathematics, Book-keeping, Shorthand, Chemistry and Music.

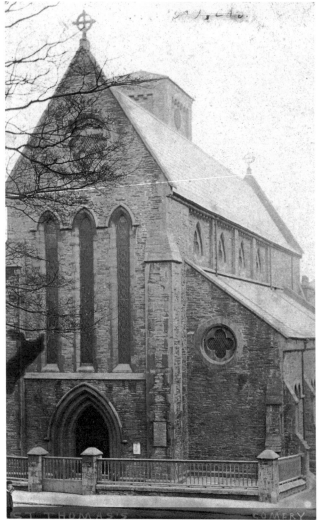

St Thomas's Church was designed by Ewan Christian, a member of the well known family of Manx architects, and was built in 1849. This picture predates a disastrous fire in 1912 which destroyed the bells, clock, chimes and organ.

Bucks Road Post Office, *c*. 1905. On the right is the Rosemount Church before the building of the spire in 1911.

This view was taken from the same spot as the one above, but facing up Rosemount. The Manx architect John Robinson was responsible for the three houses which constituted the Rosemount Hotel. The Weslyan Church, which opened in 1886, is on the left.

The new Douglas School of Art in Kensington Road was built in 1880 and its tutor was the great Manx artist John Miller Nicholson. Perhaps the most famous pupil was Archibald Knox, who attended both the old and new schools in the 1880s.

Noble's Park was established as the town's playing fields by the Noble Trustees and opened in June 1911 as part of the Coronation celebrations. The following week the island's first aeroplane flight took off from here but despite having public park status screens were set up around it so that people could be charged to see the event.

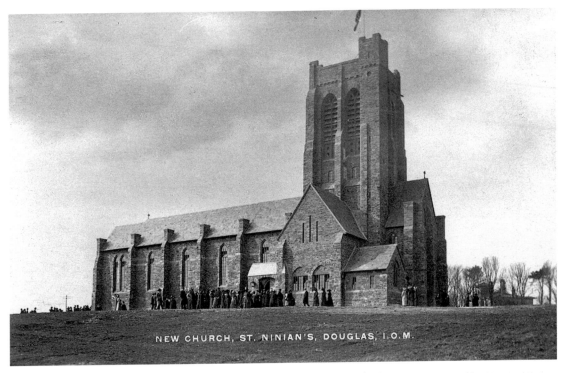

NEW CHURCH, ST. NINIAN'S, DOUGLAS, I.O.M.

From its hilltop position on Ballaquayle Road, St Ninian's Church dominates the landscape of north Douglas. This view was taken soon after its construction in 1912.

All Saints' Church on Alexandra Drive was built to fulfil a need for more church provision in the upper part of town. The church was opened in 1898 and although it was only meant to be a temporary structure it was not replaced until 1967.

Sydney Street, *c.* 1904. J. Holroyd's grocers was the only shop here and it later became Kermode & Cunningham's. The railings were very popular with children for acrobatics!

In November 1922 the scattered collections of the Manx Museum were finally gathered under one roof at the converted Noble's Hospital (built 1886). The first curator was P.M.C. Kermode, a tribute to his many years of endeavour in getting the museum established.

The Isle of Man first saw motor car racing in 1904 when trials were held to choose the British representative for the Gordon Bennett Cup competition which was to be held in France. Special laws had to be passed by the Manx parliament in order to close the appropriate roads but this was not done until just days before the first event was due to be held. However, publicity for the trials was a major success and this combined with the advantages of roads which could be easily closed led the authorities to agree to the holding of the first Tourist Trophy Race in September 1905.

In the 1907 race a new Heavy Touring Race for larger cars was inaugurated. All cars entered had to have similar specifications so that none had an unfair advantage and most, such as the Beeston Humbers above, had to have a wooden screen attached which was 5'3" wide and 6' high above the road and was intended to simulate a limousine body.

T.T. motor car races were held on the island in 1905, '06, '07, '08, '14 and '22. The race in 1905 covered the entire island but the opening and closing of too many level crossings caused innumerable problems so from 1906 onwards the familiar T.T. course emerged. In this picture, W.O. Bentley prepares for the 1914 race. He finished sixth at an average speed of 48 m.p.h.

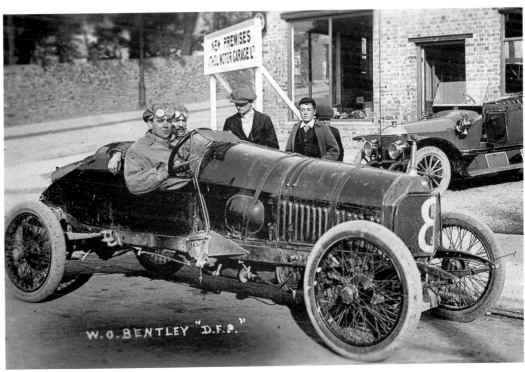

W. O. BENTLEY "D.F.P."

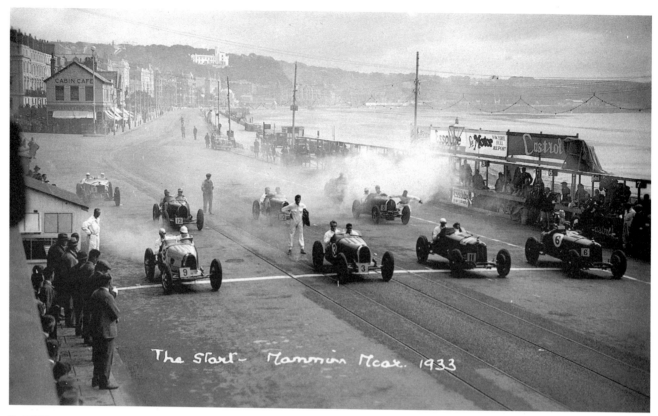

In 1933 motor car racing returned (although drivers were no longer in competition for a Tourist Trophy) and in July two races named Mannin Beg and Mannin Mooar were held on a fifty lap course which spanned Douglas and Onchan. The start was positioned in front of the Villa Marina.

The cars then proceeded up Finch Road (above), Bucks Road, Woodburne Road, and then eventually to Governor Road and down Summerhill to the promenade. The races were held again in 1934 and 1935 but lack of competitor interest and the inconveniences of staging the events led to their demise.

Following the success of the Motor Car T.T. races, the Motor Cycle T.T. was introduced in 1907. As before, the road speed limit of 20 m.p.h. and the legislation against road closure prevented the races being held in England and the island authorities were only too happy to oblige. The first course started at St Johns and preceded through Ballacraine, Kirk Michael, Peel, and back to St Johns - a lap distance of under 16 miles and a total distance of 160 miles. The first senior winner was C.R. Collier who rode a Matchless at an average speed of 38.22 m.p.h., although the result might well have been different if the runner-up had pedals on his machine also.

Stanley Woods at the start of the 1935 lightweight race. Woods was the ultimate winner, and the race was one of his ten T.T. victories between 1922 and 1939. He was also second three times, third once, and made eleven fastest laps. During his last win, the 1939 junior, he reached an average speed of over 83 m.p.h. The course used today was introduced in 1911.

Before the war sidecar events were held in 1923, 1924 and 1925, and this picture shows the 1924 winner. Boy scouts had helped in the races since 1910, performing such tasks as manning the position boards.

The Harris Promenade with the public shelter opposite the Sefton Hotel. The shelter obscured the view for traffic on the road and caused accidents due to the bend it necessitated in the tram track. Its demolition was one of the conditions for the town benefitting from the will of Henry Bloom Noble which would provide charitable trusts for hospitals, parks and other public amenities. The Pavilion Theatre next to the Sefton was built on the site of an open garden and was, for its first year, known as the Marina. It was later redeveloped to become the Gaiety.

In this view of the promenade, the bandstand used by Buxton's Pierrots is visible beyond the shelter. The promenades were the pride of the town (rather than just temporary carparks!) and although it is unusually quiet here, were often so busy that 'keep to the right' notices were displayed on the flagpoles and promenade wall.

Visit of Dr Clarke. — Garden Party at Villa Marina. June 7th 1906

At the turn of the century, the Christian Endeavour movement was sweeping the British Isles and its American founder, Dr Clarke, visited the island in June 1906. On arrival at the Victoria Pier he joined a great procession, accompanied by the Douglas Town Band, that took him to the Villa Marina. After speeches and a sit-down tea Dr Clarke went on to Ramsey, followed by hordes of supporters. Special trains had to be timetabled to carry the crowds home.

OPENING OF VILLA MARINA DOUGLAS

The Villa Marina Kursaal was opened in July 1913 by Lord and Lady Raglan who can be seen centre stage above waiting for the Douglas Town Band to strike up the national anthem. The hall had a capacity of 2000 and the stage extended out much further into the hall than today, with a pit provided for the orchestra.

L.B. Bradshaw of Finch Road and the Pierrot Village took this photograph of the Lucas Villa Marina Band. Performances were given in the gardens morning, afternoon and evening, or 'indoors if wet'. In the seasons up to the First World War (when they were promptly interned) Herr Simon Wurms's famous Imperial Viennese Band had provided the entertainment.

It was not until 1929 that Douglas Council was able to proceed with the second stage of the Villa Marina development. The promenade colonnade was completed in 1930 and the art deco arcade the following year. In the gardens, the Royal Hall was provided with a colonnade and verandah (right) giving a sheltered extension to the cafe. The fountain had to be moved to near the Broadway entrance when the Garden Room was built in the early 1970s.

The Central Promenade is rarely to be seen so crowded with pedestrians today. On the right is the Crescent Cinema, opened in 1930, and alongside it the wooden Crescent Pavilion which was erected on the Pierrot Village site. The Blue Ribands are advertised here and the Pavilion was commonly known as Buxton's. The land was offered to the Pierrots by Henry Bloom Noble when Buxton's famous troupe were forced to move from their earlier site in front of the Villa Marina.

The Palace Ballroom first opened in 1887, but was destroyed by fire both in 1906 and 1920. This picture shows the 1906 structure. The dance hall was one of the largest in Europe and a record crowd of almost 10,000, including 8000 dancers, attended the 1921 reopening.

The Palace Coliseum was opened in 1913 by opera star Vesta Tilley. Accommodation was for 3500 people and the theatre was connected to the dance hall by a covered bridge. The closing concert, starring the Bachelors, was in 1965.

The Douglas Bay Tramway opened in 1876 and the horse trams have survived to become the town's most famous feature. Above is car no. 48 of 1935 in new condition, surely one of the last horse trams to be built anywhere.

The story of Cunningham Camp is well documented in *Good Clean Fun* by Jill Drower, the great-granddaughter of the founders, Elizabeth and Joseph Cunningham. The camp was founded in 1894 at Howstrake, moving to Little Switzerland in 1904. It was, until it was sold in 1945, the most successful holiday camp in the British Isles, preceding Butlins by many years. Although it only catered for men, an average of 60,000 campers visited every year to enjoy the then unrivalled facilities and the unlimited home produced food (one camper was recorded to have eaten thirty-six egg and bacon breakfasts in one sitting).

The Pavilion games room, *c.* 1905. Joseph Cunningham is seated on the far left.

The tuck shop, available to campers who were not satisfied by the fare offered on the camp menu.

The most popular room in the camp. A sample menu says it all:

    8 - 9 a.m.,   Breakfast - porridge and milk, bacon and eggs, fresh rolls, white and brown bread, preserves, tea.
    1 - 2 p.m.,   Dinner - chicken soup, roast lamb, mint sauce, peas, potatoes, bread, preserves, tea.
    5 - 6 p.m.,   Tea - grilled sausage, roast potatoes, bread, cakes, preserves, tea.
    10 p.m.,   Supper - cheese, bread, cakes, preserves, coffee.

After these enormous meals, the dishes - up to 20,000 of them - were cleaned by specially designed dishwashers.

During the First World War the camp was used as an internment camp for men of German or Austrian extraction. Here some of the unfortunates are in the workshop making articles to be sold for charity.

This Avro 504 floatplane came over to the island in June 1914. The occasion was the Douglas Carnival Week and the plane gave pleasure trips to the winners of a Daily Mail competition.

The Regency style boarding houses of the Derby, Esplanade and Clarence Terraces were among the earliest buildings on the sea front, dating from about 1843. The Esplanade terrace of ten houses was designed by John Robinson as family houses.

One of two Avro aeroplanes that were stationed on Queen's Promenade in 1919. They provided pleasure flights and after a trip around the bay, passengers were given a souvenir brochure signed by the pilot.

The five minute flight cost one guinea, rising to three for acrobatics. Flights were dependent on the tide and whilst not in use the aeroplanes were parked on the grass alongside a tent used as a booking office. Objections by hoteliers on the Queen's Promenade that the grass could not be used by their guests or for the drying of bed linen led to the cessation of the service in 1920.

It is very likely that the earliest aerial photographs of the island to be commercially published were taken from the Avros by Robert Dowty. Robert moved to the island after gaining considerable experience in aerial photography over German East Africa during the Great War. This view of Onchan head was taken by him in 1919.

The storm of December 1924 was reported by the Liverpool *Echo* as the worst seen for years, with winds reaching hurricane force. Trees, chimney pots and tiles were strewn over the streets of Douglas and huge seas broke over Broadway. The Tower of Refuge was reported to be almost submerged by the waves.

Elizabeth Kewley and her staff outside the Crescent Post Office in 1907. The office later moved to the corner of the promenade, closing in 1989. The original building, a tea room in this picture, is now a restaurant.

Derby Castle Station, 1904, when a return fare to Ramsey would have cost half a crown. The Derby Castle buildings in the distance and the ornamental iron canopy (demolished in 1980) are much missed features of the promenade.

The plans for the development of the Howstrake Estate from 1892 included an agreement with Douglas Town Commissioners to build a promenade from Derby Castle to Port Jack - the cliff being blasted away to make room for the roadway and tram lines. Construction of the red brick houses on Royal Avenue began 1897-98. This card was published for Henry Hough, chairman of the Postcard Censorship Committee, one of whose shops can be seen to the left of the row visible here.

Port Jack enjoyed its initial popularity from the fact that mixed family bathing was allowed there at a time when Douglas beach was still strictly segregated. In recent years the bay has been subject to pollution and sees little use.

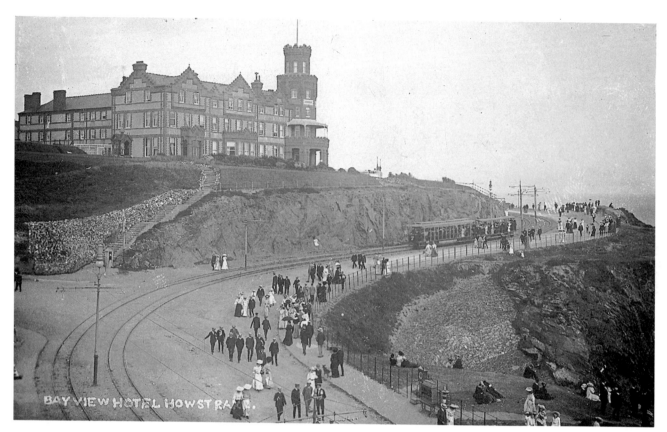

The Douglas Bay Hotel was built in 1894 and was the first customer to be supplied with electricity by the Tramways and Electric Power Company. In 1988 the hotel was destroyed by fire and the site remains undeveloped.

In 1892, before Onchan Head became just another building site, View Park Mansion was the first private house to be erected on the Howstrake Estate. Designed by Baillie Scott, it was known as the Scotch House and, much extended, became a hotel in 1920. The hotel had periods of great popularity but today lies largely empty and endangered by the possibility of demolition.

Because the hotel was a good distance from the town centre, guests were transported to and from the Victoria Pier by this superior quality courtesy bus. In this shot the 'passengers' are actually members of the hotel staff.

Onchan Commissioners first planned for the building of a Pavilion and amusement centre on Onchan Head in 1907 and as the development grew it became known as White City. The Pierrot pavilion, with Charles Harvey and the Onchans, was one of the earliest attractions. In this photograph the Toreadors are performing but by 1920 Feldman's Orphans were the entertainers.

Before the First World War, a great attraction at White City was the chance to be photographed sitting in one of the first two aeroplanes to visit the island. The Bleriot monoplane was brought over for the island's 1911 Coronation celebrations and afterwards remained as it was impounded during a financial dispute with the owner, George Barnes.

Developed by Alderman Stephen Quirk and J.P. Smith, proprietor of the Metropole Hotel, the figure-eight roller coaster was probably White City's biggest attraction. Originally made of wood, it was rebuilt in steel after suffering from rot.

The Howstrake Golf Links date back to 1894, although after the First World War a completely new course was developed between the original hilltop location and Harbour Road. The clubhouse was originally on King Edward Road, but by 1935, when this card was published, the building had been relocated at Harbour Road.

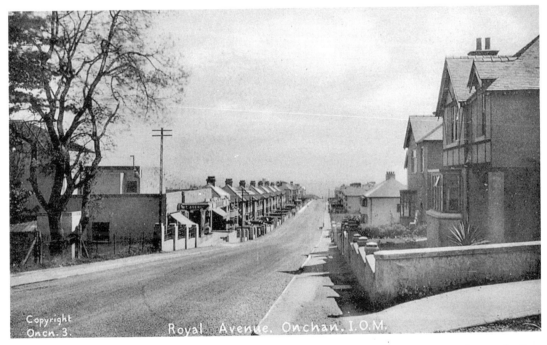

Royal Avenue, 1937, with the newly opened Avenue Cinema on the left (it became Skillicorn's warehouse in the 1960s). The Avenue was built in 1898 to connect the village with the new developments at Port Jack, but for many years the only buildings on the left were the Village Hall and the Howstrake Mill. The Mill was demolished in the 1930s to make way for the new houses shown above.

Governor's Bridge carries the old road over the Glencrutchery Valley and is best known today as a vantage point on the T.T. course. For many years the Cunningham Camp had a stand here for the use of the campers during the racing.

The grey painted houses on Governor's Road were first occupied in 1897. Terraces in Onchan were given different names and were numbered separately even when on the same road; in this stretch they were named Sunnyside, Seaview, Woodside and Clifton Terraces. The Main Road and Governor's Road were gradually built up and the thatched roofs and quaint outside staircases on the older properties disappeared. These staircases were sometimes marked with chalk circles to protect them from the fairies.

During the 1930s many territorial units, mostly from Liverpool, passed through Onchan on the way to their summer camps at Bibaloe. Bibaloe was named after a ford at the bottom of the White Bridge Hill and Bibaloe Glen leads up from Groudle to the Clypse Reservoir. Here the troops march along Main Road, *c.* 1936.

Main Road soon after the opening of the Co-op in 1934. On the right is the new branch of the Isle of Man Bank which was built that year on the site of the Manx Arms' bowling green. The Manx Arms opened in 1827.

Onchan Butt, 1906. Molly Carooin's eighteenth century cottage is on the left, and in the right foreground the old Parish School, built in 1845. The lamp standard was one of five supplied in 1897 and together they provided the first electric lighting on the island. Dominating the scene is St Peter's Church, built in 1833; the previous church on the site dated back to the twelfth century and was where Captain Bligh of *The Bounty* was married.

This postcard of Forrest Lodge dates from 1910, when a holiday in Onchan would still have been a quiet, country affair. The writer of the card says that they are becoming 'more infatuated with the place every day and with dear Captain Quinn, the proprietor.' The lodge was by Mill House at the top end of Molly Quirk's Glen.

Areas known as 'Abbeylands' are still to be found around Onchan and Lonan, and also once existed in the parishes of Rushen, Malew, Braddan and German. They were lands belonging to Rushen Abbey, which also controlled the leasing of all the property on them. Onchan Abbeylands post office (right) was in business between 1898 and 1941 and run by the Leece family.

Harvesting at Ballacrink, Onchan. Before the First World War tractors were a rare sight on British farms and most farm work was done either by horses or traction engines. Here, such an engine is powering a threshing mill and bailer. The farm worker on the left has his trousers tied at the knee to stop longtails running up his legs.

Joseph Cunningham moved his camp to the larger Victoria Road site in 1904, although the Howstrake camp above Groudle continued to be used until 1973. It remained largely under canvas until the main building programme began in 1937 and during the War was used as a base for the Royal Marines.

The Manx Electric Railway was the most popular means of reaching the camp and this stone shelter was built about 1910. Constructed and maintained by the camp rather than the railway company, its remains still survive today, although the stop is now rarely used. This photograph was taken before the building developments of the 1930s when the intake of campers was restricted to males only.

This unusual view of Groudle Station shows the MER shelter at the glen which was restored for the centenary celebrations in 1993. The photograph shows the original line of track as it existed for the short 1893 season when the single track came much closer to the hotel to form a turning loop.

G. Dobie's Refreshment Rooms at Groudle. The cafe building had originally been the pavilion at the end of the Iron Pier in Douglas, and was moved to Groudle when the pier was dismantled in 1893. The Groudle cafe was in business for many years and even published its own postcards of the area.

Still a feature of Groudle, the water wheel and wheel house were operational by 1895. The wheel provided power for the glen's electricity and fairy lights, and water was also pumped from here to the Groudle Hotel.

Groudle Glen's dance pavilion was an open-air structure reached by a bridge near Mona Grose's sweet and postcard stall. Music was provided by a small band performing twice daily in the afternoons and evenings.

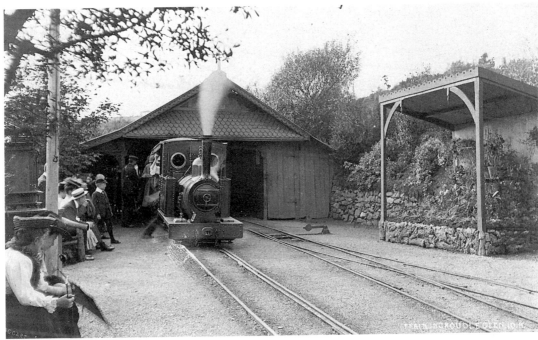

1996 is the centenary year of the Groudle Glen Railway. It closed in 1962 but due to the hard work of the Isle of Man Steam Railway Supporters Association (who actually rebuilt it) it reopened in the 1980s. Most passengers used the railway to get to the headland zoo and cafe and here a complement of them have boarded the locomotive *Sea Lion* at Lhen Coan station.

At Sea Lion Rocks passengers got off at the station next to the zoo and followed this path to the walkways which traversed the rocks, giving the best views of the sea lions. The Sea Lion Cafe is on the hilltop.

For many years the sea lion keeper at Groudle was Gaby Dobson, who lived with his family in a stone house on the beach. Originally, eleven sea lions had been sent from California, but only six survived the journey and after the First World War only Tommy and Jenny (who did most of the tricks) remained. Besides bringing visitors, the electric railway also transported the eighteen stones of fish that the sea lions ate each week.

Other animals kept at Groudle prior to 1914 included polar bears and two brown bear cubs. They were obtained by the proprietor in Manchester and, chained to rocks without shelter, were not his zoo's most humane attraction. There was also an aviary at Groudle.

The Liverpool Arms Hotel has always advertised itself as the original half-way house on the way to Laxey from Douglas. It was first mentioned in Leech's Guide of 1861, which noted its accomm– odation for horses, an unusual feature at a time when travellers on the island's roads were rare. The hotel became the focal point for a sparsely populated area and with the coming of the electric railway, one of the original letter boxes to be emptied by the conductors was positioned here.

The development of the area between the wars is evident in this 1930s view of Baldrine. Newly built bungalows such as these indicated the growth in commuter and retirement homes in formerly rural areas.

The village of Garwick, *c.* 1914. The shop on the right also served as a post office and in 1915 Mary Caine became postmistress, a position she held for fifty-four years. In the 1920s the building acquired its familiar veranda.

At the height of its popularity, Garwick Glen boasted attractions ranging from a fairy pool and maze to the ruins of a whisky still. Boats could also be hired to visit the nearby sea caves, one of which could be followed for more than 200 feet to an oil lamp which was kept burning at the end.

The Hermit's Archway at Garwick. The bay has many interesting rock formations and caves, and before the Revestment Act of 1765 smugglers, later made famous in Sir Walter Scott's *Guy Mannering,* made use of these.

This photograph shows saloon car no. 6 of 1894 climbing the gradient from Laxey to South Cape. The card dates from before the 1898 conversion from Hopkinson bow collectors (similar to those used on Snaefell today) to trolley pole operation as a means of gathering power. The steep climb out of Laxey illustrates why the coastal line was not suitable for steam traction.

The Commercial Hotel survives to this day as the Coach and Horses on New Road, Laxey. It was once the busiest inn in the village, with stabling for one hundred horses. However, by the time of this photograph the premises had to deal with motor travellers as well.

Valentines reissued this card of the dining hall in Laxey Glen Gardens to commemorate its destruction by fire in August 1913. The owner, Robert Williamson, was widely travelled and the restaurant was built in Swiss style. In the early days of the Glen Gardens Williamson brought over famous personalities such as the tight-rope walker Blondin, and General Tom Thumb the midget.

The hobby horse and swings at Glen Gardens. Other attractions included the boating lake and grounds for bowls, croquet and tennis. Dances and concerts were held on the dance floor in front of the pavilion and the boating lake could also be drained for open-air dances.

Situated on the southern slopes of the Laxey Glen, Axnfel dates from 1884 and served as a sanatorium and a guest house before being converted into a youth hostel in 1962. The hostel was particularly popular with school groups but nonetheless closed in 1985, although plans have recently been made to refurbish and reopen the building. This photograph shows Axnfel as a guest house, c. 1905.

Laxey Harbour, 1905. Zinc ore from the nearby mines was kept in the walled store while awaiting shipment and the little stone building adjacent to it (now a cafe and shelter) was used to store the more valuable lead ore. Today's promenade and sea wall were constructed in the 1930s.

In 1875, at the height of their success, the Laxey mines employed 662 workers and produced 20% of the zinc mined in the British Isles, plus important quantities of lead and silver. Wagons ran to the quay and emptied directly into the holds of vessels such as the Monk coasters of Liverpool. The eighteenth century bridge was part of the original coastal road.

Laxey Valley, with the partly rebuilt Laxey Car Depot, centre right, which fell victim to fire in April 1930. Probably started by a burning cigarette, the fire resulted in the loss of four motor cars and other equipment. The new depot is still in use today.

King Orry's grave is the remains of the largest megalithic monument on the island. Although not the resting place of the King Orry of Manx history, it is a burial place for chieftains dating from around 2000 BC. The site is situated near Minorca MER station on the Ballaragh Road but has now been cut through by a roadway and partially built over.

Laxey Post Office was run for a long time by the Kelly family and was one of several shops in the old village before the war. The cafe next to the post office later became Fred Osborne Printers.

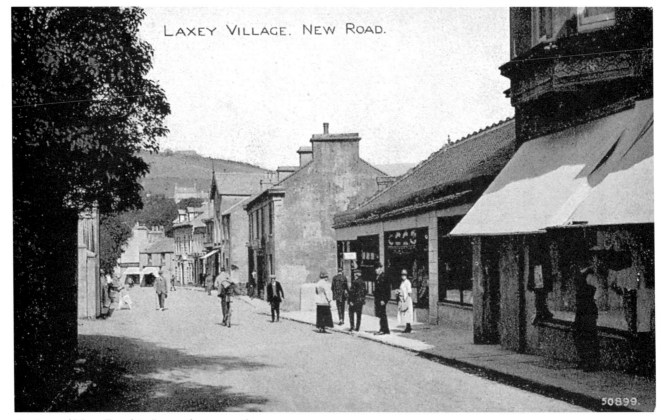

A view of New Road in Laxey between the wars.

In September 1930 the Isle of Man was devastated by the worst storms in living memory. In the south, the buildings of Port Erin were flooded and the steam railway was badly affected with the station yard, workshops, and the line to Braddan all under water. However, the worst flooding was in Glen Auldyn and Laxey.

Some of the residents of Glen Road, many of whom had to fight for hours in total darkness against the waters that threatened to engulf their homes. Practically every home between Holroyd's Mill and the harbour was affected, walls were swept away and a huge cavity was torn in Main Road. Untold damage was done to the contents of the houses and some inhabitants found themselves in serious danger, only to be rescued through their windows at the last moment.

During the flood a twenty yard portion of the quay at Laxey harbour was split to its foundations, causing many tons of stone to crash into the quayside. The harbour board forbade villagers from dumping waste back in the river for fear that it would be washed into the harbour where it would cause an obstruction. 'It came from the river and into the river it ought to go' was the blunt response from the villagers.

At the Laxey Wheel, four of the arches which carried the pumping shaft across the river were washed away and for a while it seemed that the wheel would never work again. The mines changing house also collapsed and a boiler weighing five tons was carried down the river a distance of fifty yards.

This view of Laxey Station, *c.* 1909, shows car no. 27. It was a converted crossbench trailer popularly known as a paddlebox due to the wider footboards needed to keep feet clear of the axleboxes. Laxey Station was built on the village green and two of the rustic kiosks still survive, although the large restaurant in the background was destroyed by fire in September 1917. In the distance is the Mine Captain's house, now the Mines Tavern.

Christ Church, Laxey, was completed in 1856. The Laxey Wheel was also put into service that year and both owed their construction to the lead and silver mining industry which was thriving at the time. Although Lonan Parish Church was over three miles away, Christ Church was only built after considerable

opposition from the vicar was overcome. It was erected on part of the grounds of the house of William Rowe, Captain of the Mines, who allowed a public right of way through his garden to the church.

The white buses of Manx Motors and the red of Manxland Bus Service Ltd originally used the entrance to Laxey Glen Gardens for the halfway stop between Ramsey and Douglas. However, by the 1930s a proper bus station, now a car showroom, was in operation for Isle of Man Road Services Ltd. The buses waiting at the station are a 1927 Leyland Lion PLSC1 and a 1935 Leyland Lion LT7.

The Laxey Mine was still working when this 1927 photograph was taken, although the washing floors visible in the background soon fell silent after the death of owner Robert Williamson that year. One of the shops on the right was an ironmonger's run by his brother David Williamson, although the Avondale Cafe may be more fondly remembered by generations of holiday makers. Crossbench motor cars, such as those in the foreground, are still in use but have become an unusual sight north of Laxey in recent years.

GREAT LAXEY MINES, I.O.M.

The majority of the mine buildings in this 1904 view of
Mines Road have been demolished. However, out of
view to the left, 'Ham and Egg' terrace still survives.
Apart from visitors to the wheel, this was also the half-
way stop for horse-drawn coaches to and from
Douglas and the 1/- dinners served by most of the
houses on the terrace were extremely popular. The
building on the left was a corn mill, later part of an
engineering works.

An unusual view of the Laxey Wheel - from the inside.
The segments of the wheel are connected to the central
hub by two sets of twenty-four wooden arms and four
sets of twenty-four tie rods. The cross tie rods, which
are fixed to each other at the crossing point, are visible
just below the central hub.

Agneash from Rencell, Laxey, I.O.M.

Agneash village, situated to the north of Laxey at the head of Glen Mooar, seen from Rencell Hill. Agneash was known locally as 'The City' and its Woollen Fair was once famous throughout the island. The village also had a mine with a wheel similar to (but smaller than) the Lady Isabella. The mine's Dumbells shaft was the richest in the whole area, but although the Agneash shaft (sunk 1850) and the Corner shaft (1862) were successful, by 1887 all the machinery had been dismantled and the mine left to flood.

The six cars of the Snaefell Mountain Railway were built in 1895 by G.F. Milnes of Birkenhead and are still in use today. Here, a group of motormen, conductors and engineers pose with car no. 6 on the track leading into Snaefell car sheds, c. 1905.

SNAEFELL FROM THE BUNGALOW, I.O.M.

The popular Bungalow Hotel was built in 1896 to replace a shelter on the Mountain Road crossing known as the Halfway Hut. Much of the hotel's custom was provided by the coach service to Tholt-y-Will which was discontinued in the 1950s. As a result of this the hotel was closed and demolished in 1958.

The recently completed summit station of the Mountain Railway, c. 1895. The wooden catwalk in the foreground led to the original Snaefell Summit Hotel which was not fully developed until 1900. When the hotel burnt down, the station was also removed and today's castellated building was erected to serve both functions in 1906.

SUMMIT SNAEFELL MOUNTAIN, 2034 FT ABOVE SEA LEVEL.

The view of the summit and railway from the roof of the new Snaefell Summit Hotel, *c.* 1935.

Mr A. Davidson, official guide to Snaefell Summit, stands behind these ladies, photographed *c.* 1906. His job was to describe the views to tourists, charging them a penny each for the pleasure, and he appeared in most of the souvenir postcards of the summit. These were often stamped with a special cachet, recording a visitor's trip to the mountain top.

The development of Sulby Glen as a tourist attraction was boosted by a motor charabanc service from the Bungalow to Tholt-y-Will which was operated by the Manx Electric Railway Co. from 1907. Not all the visitors could afford to travel in the style of this motorist, but the Mill View Tea Gardens and the Carrick Mountain resort in the glen were very popular with the excursionists.

A group photograph in the glen formed part of the MER's conducted tours. The smallest boy in the party usually had the privilege of wearing the guide's cap for the occasion.

The waterfall on the Glen Darragh River and the road leading up to the two Ballaquine farms (the Overfarm and the Near) are visible on the left of this photograph. The farm buildings belong to the North Star and little has changed today. At one time they were popular as an inn, offering overnight accommodation for travellers at the time this picture was taken.

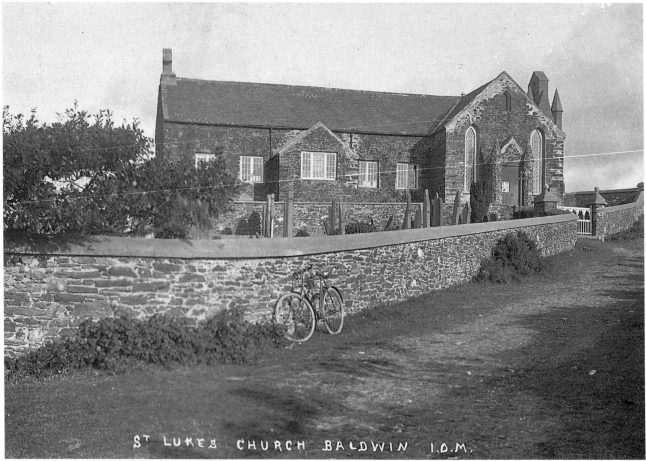

St Luke's Church in Baldwin was built in 1836 with the unusual feature of a chimney in the shape of a cross. The chimney was required as the building also served as a school until the East Baldwin Board School was opened in the 1870s. The schoolroom was separated from the consecrated part of the building by a sliding partition and was later used as the church's social room.

West Baldwin before construction of the Baldwin reservoir. This development was made necessary as the existing reservoirs at Clypse and Kerroodhoo, although holding a combined 75 million gallons, were unable to cope with the ever growing population of Douglas. When completed, Baldwin could hold over 300 million gallons, more than enough to meet demand until recently. The figure in the foreground is that of local man William Stanley Cavell, who worked on the construction scheme.

The New Douglas-Reservoir at Injebreck.

Commencing in 1900, construction of the reservoir took five years. Most of the area seen here behind the 300ft embankment was submerged, including the road and cottages to the left. In the foreground of this photograph one of the steam engines used on the works railway is moving stone used to line the outer face of the embankment. The white building in the distance was the pavilion at Injebreck Pleasure Grounds.

A weir on the River Glass at Tromode, just below Cronkbourne House and upstream from the disused Tromode Mill. The town of Douglas derives its name from the meeting of the River Dhoo and the River Glass. Tromode is the birthplace of the artist Archibald Knox.

Opened in 1854, Crosby Post Office was originally housed in an outbuilding which was behind the Wagon and Horses Inn. The Gelling family have run the office as part of a general store since 1891 and at the time of this view, c. 1914, local resident Hall Caine was a regular customer.

In 1905 the traffic passing through Crosby was still exclusively horse-dawn, although there was rather more of it than when the railway had arrived in the 1870s. The only regular traffic then consisted of four coaches per day passing between Peel and Douglas, plus the deep vermilion mail gig and two locally owned carrier carts.

Crosby Station was never particularly busy and the small goods shed was demolished in the 1960s, well before the closure of the line. The station was in a very attractive tree–lined setting ideal for starting country walks, although the manure siding was never a popular spot.

The Crosby Hotel dates from before 1825 and the building was known as York Cottage until 1863. The hotel is now a popular viewpoint on the T.T. course.

The Highlander, Crosby, was a small country inn at the foot of the Greeba Mountain on the main Douglas-Peel road. Built as a dwelling house in 1840, it was licenced in 1862. The house was annually the focus of the evening celebrations held by the locals to mark Candlemass Day (2nd February).

When this photograph was taken, Ballavagher House was being used as a youth hostel and was evidently in need of repair. The Gelling family sold the estate in 1964 and the new owners finally renovated the building. The house is around 200 years old and was probably built by the Gellings, but the surrounding farm and outbuildings are much older.

"BALLAVAGHER HOUSE" (YHA) UNION MILLS, ISLE OF MAN.   DBH

ST TRINIAN'S CHURCH, MAROWN, CROSBY, I.O.M.

The roofless fourteenth century St Trinian's Chapel stands on the Douglas-Peel road, west of Crosby, and this view shows the church after the north wall was rebuilt by the Museum Trustees in 1908. In folklore the chapel is associated with the legend of the buggane who would not allow the building to be roofed. However, a more likely explanation is that it was owned by a Scottish order around the time when Scots were being violently expelled from the island by Sir William Montacute in 1343.

Although close to new developments such as the Mount Murray Golf Course, the area around the Braaid is still one of the most remote regions of the island. The Braaid's Young Men's Club was established in the hall (centre) in 1937 and is still going today. The hall is now best known for the annual Braaid Eisteddfod.

Mount Murray is a mansion situated on Richmond Hill, about four miles from Douglas on the Castletown road. Built as Moor Hall in 1736, it was originally the home of Governor Murray and later passed into the ownership of his relative, the Duke of Atholl, who lived there between 1793 and 1830. The house was well-known for its fine gardens, as can be seen in this view from the 1930s when it was in use as a hotel.

Glen Darragh suffered badly in the great storms of September 1930 and inhabitants of this cottage near the mill awoke in the middle of the night to find water swirling around their beds and furniture floating in the kitchen. They, like some of the residents of Laxey, had to be rescued through a window.

The road from Glen Darragh meets the main Douglas-Peel road at Glen Vine, an area which was also affected by the floods. Much building development has taken place since this photograph was taken and it is likely that these boys represented the village's entire youth population at the time.

The Dalrymple Memorial Chapel in Union Mills was built in 1862 from a design by John Robertson, architect of the Douglas Court House and Peveril Hotel. The chapel was closed in 1973 and became a grain store.

Union Mills' first post office opened in 1853, but only moved to the village shop, shown here, in 1932. The shop was built and run by the Green family from 1869 and amongst other functions it also served as a small lending library.